Dino-Splashing

Written and illustrated by Steve Smallman

"Last one in is a dirty dinosaur!" shouted Nutter. He ran down to the water with Flapper and Stretch. But instead of splashing into the water...

they fell into thick mud.

SPLAT!

"What's going on?" asked Nutter. "Where's the water?"

"Look!" said Stretch. "The waterfall. It's not working anymore!"

"But I need a shower!" said Flapper.

"Yes," said Nutter. "You are a bit muddy! Let's get our water back!"

An old dinosaur was stretching her neck up to look for the water. Stretch and Nutter ran along her back, right to the top of the waterfall. Flapper flew up to meet them.

They ran along the riverbed. Flapper kept stopping to gobble up all the fish.

Then, they came to a dead end. A large pile of rocks was blocking the river.

"We'll never move the rocks," said Nutter.

Just then Stretch spotted an enormous, wobbly rock on the hill.

"Come with me, Nutter. I've got a plan!" Stretch shouted.

"**BURP!**" said Flapper.

“If we can push this rock down the hill,” said Stretch, “it will smash the pile of rocks and let the water back into the river!”

So Nutter ran at the huge rock... but it didn’t move.

The noise woke up a huge tyrannosaurus rex. The T-rex spotted Flapper.

"Yummy!" he shouted. He ran towards Flapper!

Flapper got out of the way just in time. The huge rock went tumbling down the hill, with the T-rex hanging onto it!

With a **CRASH** the pile of rocks went flying, and the water came gushing back into the riverbed.

“We did it!” cried Stretch. “We got our water back and got rid of old Fangface, too!”

But he spoke too soon.

With a roar, the T-rex got up.

They were trapped. Stretch and Nutter could not run away, and Flapper was too full to fly.

"Flapper, hang on to my neck!" said Stretch. "Come on, Nutter!"

The T-rex was about to charge...

so Nutter, Stretch and Flapper took a leap into the river! The river swept them along and they left the angry T-rex far behind.

"That was easy," said Nutter.

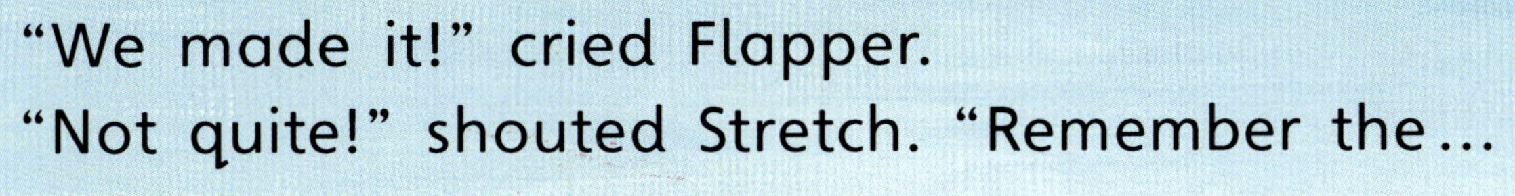

“We made it!” cried Flapper.
“Not quite!” shouted Stretch. “Remember the...

Waterfaaaalllllll!"

Nutter, Flapper and Stretch got out of the water.

"I need to lie down," said Stretch.

"I feel sick," groaned Flapper.

"That was fun!" cried Nutter. "Let's do it again!"